Positive Affirmation Alphabet Book for Smart Kids

Learning ABC the Fun Way While Building Your Children's Confidence and Empowering Them With Gratitude and a Positive Mindset

By Aileen Jarvis

sources. Please consult a licensed professional before attempting any techniques outlined in this book.

By reading this document, the reader agrees that under no circumstances is the author responsible for any losses, direct or indirect, that are incurred as a result of the use of the information contained within this document, including, but not limited to, errors, omissions, or inaccuracies.

Contents

Introduction

Do you remember the days where you used to recite, "A is for apple, B is for bird, C is for cat…"? Well, it's time to say goodbye to the old way of learning the ABC's.

In this book, your child will learn alphabets in a way that not only enhance their literacy but also boost their self-confidence and empower their positive mindset. This book is divided into three sections. Each section contains A-Z positive affirmation phrases ranging from short and simple ones to more complex ones.

Words have an incredible ability to shape people's experiences and outlook of the world around them—especially in young children. As parents, you are probably familiar with the concept of daily affirmation. Affirmations are short mantras we can repeat to ourselves to create a more positive mindset. Turns out, affirmations are not just for adults. It can be a powerful tool for children as well!

Positive affirmations can help children develop positive self-talk, which is one of the crucial foundations for positive thinking skill. Having a positive mindset not only improve our overall well-being but also help us manage stress and make better decisions.

By developing a positive mindset, children can learn to be more confident in themselves and work towards their individual potentials.

Are you ready to help your child discover a more empowering way of learning the ABC's?

Let's do it!

The Easy ABC's of Positive Affirmation for Beginner

A is for

Awesome

I am awesome.

B is for

Blessed

I am blessed.

C is for

Confident

I am confident

____

____

____

____

D is for

Dependable

I am dependable.

E is for

Energetic

I am energetic.

F is for

Friendly

I am friendly.

G is for

Grateful

I am grateful.

____

____

____

H is for

Healthy

I am healthy.

____

____

____

____

I is for

Imaginative

I am imaginative.

____

____

____

J is for

Joyous

I am joyous.

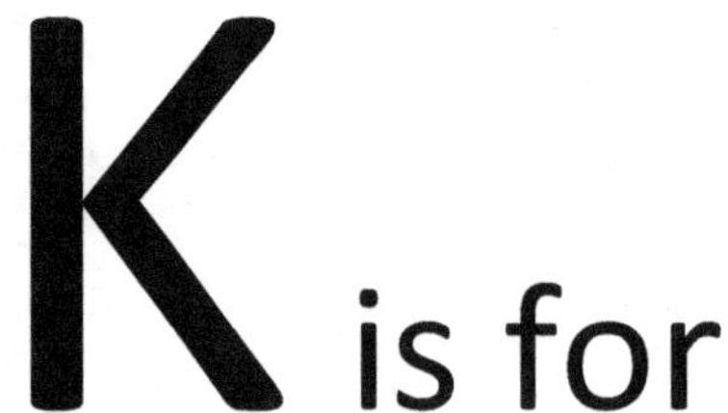 **K** is for

Kind

I am kind.

____

____

____

L is for

Loving

I am loving.

____

____

____

____

M is for

Mindful

I am mindful.

N is for

Neat

I am neat.

O is for

Outstanding

I am outstanding.

P is for

Patient

I am patient.

Q is for

Quick-witted

I am quick-witted.

R is for

Respectful

I am respectful.

S is for

Strong

I am strong.

T is for

Thoughtful

I am thoughtful.

____

____

____

U is for

Unique

I am Unique

V is for

Vibrant

I am vibrant.

____

____

____

____

W

is for

Wonderful

I am wonderful.

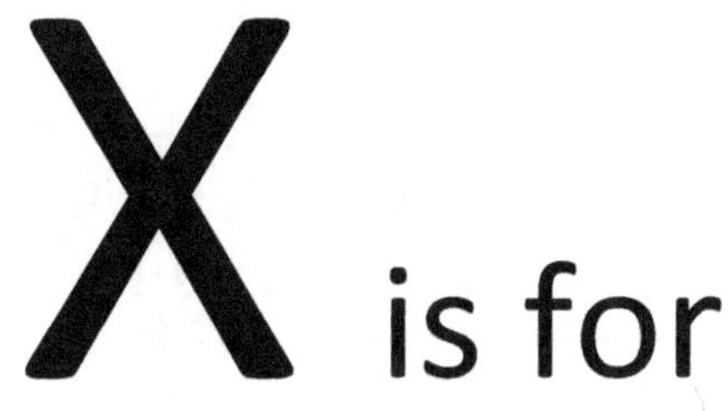 is for

Extraordinary

I am extraordinary.

____

____

____

Y is for

Youthful

I am youthful.

____

____

____

____

Z is for

Zealous

I am zealous.

More ABC's of Positive Affirmation for Intermediate Learner

A is for

Abundant

I feel abundant.

B is for

Beautiful

I am beautiful inside and out.

C is for

Creative

I find creative ways to solve problems.

____

____

____

____

D is for

Diversity

I appreciate diversity.

____

____

____

E is for

Excited

I am always excited to learn new things.

F is for

Faith

My faith is bigger than my fear.

____

____

____

____

G is for

Grateful

I am grateful for my family.

H is for

Help

I enjoy helping others.

I is for

Impossible

Impossible means I'm possible!

____

____

____

J is for

Just

I love myself just as I am.

K is for

Knowledge

Knowledge is power.

L is for

Laughter

Life is better when I am laughing.

M is for

is for

Meaningful

I live a meaningful life.

N is for

New

My mind is filled with new ideas.

O is for

Opportunity

I see opportunity everywhere I go.

P is for

Positive

I have a positive outlook.

Q is for

Question

It is better to ask a question than not to know.

R is for

Radiate

I radiate happiness.

S is for

Success

The key to success is discipline.

____

____

____

____

T is for

Talent

Every person is born with talent.

U is for

Unbeatable

I have an unbeatable mindset.

V is for

Vulnerable

I accept my vulnerabilities as part of my growth.

____

____

____

____

W is for

Winner

Winner takes chances and never gives up.

X is for

Excellence

Excellence is a habit—the things what we repeatedly do.

____

____

____

____

Y is for

Year

I am becoming a better version of myself every year.

____

____

____

____

Z is for

Zappy

Zappy songs make me happy.

The Positive Affirmation ABC's for Advanced Learner

A is for

Appreciate

I appreciate all the blessings in my life.

____

____

____

____

B is for

Brave

I am brave and bold in the pursuit of my dream.

C is for

Compassionate

I am compassionate toward others and myself.

D is for

Driven

I am driven to be the best version of myself.

E is for

Enough

I am enough and will always be.

F is for

Forgive

I forgive myself and others for their mistakes.

____

____

____

____

G is for

Good

I believe there is so much good in the world.

H is for

Humble

I am humble and let my action speaks
for itself.

I is for

Invest

I invest my time and energy on things that help me grow.

J is for

Joyful

I choose to be joyful at this moment.

K is for

Kindness

Kindness begins with me.

L is for

Love

I am loved, loving, and lovable.

M is for

Mistakes

Mistakes help me grow and learn.

N is for

Never

I never give up on my dream.

____

____

____

____

O is for

Open

I am open to the possibilities in life.

P is for

Purpose

I live a life of purpose.

____

____

____

____

Q is for

Quality

I always do quality work.

R is for

Resilient

I am resilient.

S is for

Strength

Asking for help is a sign of strength, not weakness.

____

____

____

____

T is for

Truth

I live in my truth, and I am true to my feelings.

____

____

____

U is for

Unconditional

I love and accept myself unconditionally.

V is for

Value

My value doesn't decrease based on someone's inability to see my worth.

W

is for

Worthy

I am worthy of the life I want to live.

X is for

Excel

I excel in everything I set my heart to do.

____

____

____

____

Y is for

Yes

I say "Yes!" to opportunities in life.

____

____

____

____

Z is for

Zesty

I always have a zest for life and adventure.
